9781646711734

Totem Guardians Oracle Deck
By Tanya Bond

Copyright © 2023 U.S. Games Systems, Inc.

All rights reserved. The illustrations, cover design, and contents are protected by copyright. No part of this book may be reproduced in any graphic, electronic or mechanical form including photocopying, recording, taping or by any information storage retrieval system without permission in writing from the publisher, except by a reviewer who wishes to quote brief passages in connection with a review for inclusion in a print publication or online platform.

10 9 8 7 6 5 4 3 2 1

Made in China

Published by
U.S. GAMES SYSTEMS, INC.
179 Ludlow Street • Stamford, CT 06902 USA
www.usgamesinc.com

Introduction

I created the Totem Guardians Oracle Deck during a period of my life when I was forced to face my shadow side, with all its hidden emotions and deep-seated beliefs. All the old stuffed feelings that I had been carrying around since childhood came out to the surface, one after another. As I was facing and integrating all these different facets of my personality, all the past selves, I explored what kind of messages I would have liked to receive that could make this journey a little bit easier and lighter. For the visual inspiration I decided to turn to the natural world of fauna. Some of the animals that I chose are common, others are unusual, and some are mythical or imaginary. Some are depicted with their human companions, others by themselves, and some appear in the form of a shapeshifter. The message in each card resonates with the archetypal energy of the animal it represents, the way it appears and behaves. Unlike most oracle decks, these cards are not meant to foretell your future, but rather bring you into a state of peace with the present moment and encourage you to contemplate your life from the neutral position of an observer. I recommend that you only pick one card at a time and sit with the message, exploring how it resonates with what you are going through on a given day.

— Tanya Bond
(aka Tatiana Bondareva)

The Cards
1 · Nightingale Music

The nightingale card is a reminder to acknowledge the role music plays in your life. Notice the way one tune affects you, whether it lifts you up or strongly resonates with what you are already feeling inside. If you have an urge to listen to a song on the spur of the moment, or you wake up with a tune on your mind—play it! See if there is a message for you in the lyrics of the song, or an energetic resonance in the melody. Both of these synchronicities will connect you more with your present state of feeling and bring deeper awareness to it. Singing, dancing, playing music, or listening to live as well as recorded music will also uplift you when you really need to raise your vibration. Or, if in need of a good cry, a sad melody and lyrics can help you get to the tipping point of connecting with your current emotion.

2 · Whale
Resonance

The whale spirit animal reminds us to be consciously aware of the way the outside world reacts in resonance to the frequency that we are emitting through habitual feelings and beliefs about how things really are. Dare to change this cause and effect, not via bypassing any negative frequency that's already sitting inside you; but instead by noticing it, acknowledging that it's in you, communicating with it, allowing it to pass through you without resistance and emitting a different frequency once the work is done. Should the echoes of old programs reassert themselves again, be willing to release yet another layer of them. For some of this negative programming is deep seated and has been passed on to you from generations of people reinforcing and resisting, and therefore affirming these negative frequencies. Integrate these feelings by allowing them to pass through you. Give them your conscious attention instead of plunging into the story that brought them about. Direct this valuable energy build-up with your inward focus by releasing it through tears or anger, motion or stillness and breathing, whatever feels most suitable in the moment. When it's time, consciously replace it with an outlook that feels good and resonates with what you really want to see in your world.

3 · Frog
Dream World

The frog is our messenger between the dimensions we visit in our dreams and this realm. Make your dreams more vivid and memorable by keeping a dream journal. Look for solutions to your current troubles either in past dreams or the future ones. Declare an intention before going to sleep to get a hint within your dream as to how to resolve your problem, or to help you integrate a repetitive old pattern that you can't seem to shake off yet. A more down-to-earth message from the frog is to make sure you get enough sleep. Enough does not mean what is prescribed for an average human; but enough for the way you feel right now even if some of the responsibilities and daily tasks might get disrupted by it.

4 · Goat
Resistance

The goat totem speaks about resistance. Not all resistance is equal, but if you picked this card you will know what kind it is in reference to. Resisting what is only creates more of the circumstances that you are trying to avoid. Resistance causes a lot of internal suffering, for your gaze is securely stuck on avoiding something that you do not want to see. The energy of resistance is not congruent with the energy of achieving something better. Finding a neutral balance within, while maintaining softer energy toward what's happening on the outside will ensure that your emotional energy is not used to perpetuate the current circumstances, but rather flow through them in grace. What if what you are experiencing was okay? What if you nurtured the feeling, that what is—is ok, and has a place and reason to be? Nothing is ever stagnant; everything changes, and your current situation will also pass. Try to drop the resistance to the present moment and instead flow with what is, towards your goal, in a slow and steady pace. Stop wasting your energy on resistance, and see if circumstances come to change right before your eyes.

5 · Snowy Owl
Judgement

The owl totem invites us to look into the paradigm of judgement. Being judgemental of other people's choices, actions, way of life, judging where they are saying and doing the wrong things implies that we know better what's best for them. It suggests that we absolutely do not trust in the wisdom of their path. Looking back on your life you might remember that even the wrong turns would sometimes bring you to the right place—and so it is for everyone. Therefore, judging others and trying to fix them or their life has no purpose. This energy would be better spent on yourself and guiding your own life to the best outcomes as you see them. Lead by example if you feel called to do so, or share your thoughts if invited, but otherwise try to allow others to be who they are, flaws and all. Allow them to make their mistakes and proceed on their journey, for it is as valid as yours.

6 · Bunny
Self-talk

The bunny card asks you to check on your internal self-talk. We often judge, we blame, we shame, we belittle, we discourage and we diminish ourselves worse than anyone out there ever could, and it hurts just as deeply. The little child inside of us hears all these hurtful words and all it wants to do is hide and cry and never come out to play. This is how we slowly but surely destroy our potential for joy, creativity and adventure. Show yourself acceptance, no matter what you did or didn't do, or what you think is wrong with you. Show yourself kindness despite all the perceived mistakes and wrong-doings, just like you would to a little child who just stumbled and is upset. Show yourself compassion and most importantly LOVE.

7 · Unicorn
Uniqueness

The unicorn reminds you about the inherent magic within you. There's no one else out there in the world who is exactly like you. No one else has your unique talents and abilities, no matter how trivial they might seem to you. You are the only one who has had your experiences that give you a special perspective only you can see. You are the sole owner of your wonderful weirdness and quirks and the world needs you to be you. It's hard sometimes to see yourself as an amazing expression of life because you've been you all your life and it's hard to see anything special in something so familiar. You observe others and you love how amazing some people in your life are. Yet remember that other people also see you as an amazing human and appreciate how unique and different you are. Let your internal uniqueness blossom, by accepting every part of yourself and every part of your journey that has helped shape you further. Let yourself shine and share your true self with the world.

8 · Red-crowned Crane
Family Beliefs

The red-crowned crane totem invites us to look into our family programs; those ideas, beliefs, views and expectations that we inherited from our long family line. We embraced many of these views, no questions asked, at an age when we simply accepted everything that came from authority figures in our life. Look through the prism of your higher self at these ideas on how you expect things should be. Consider what is manifesting in your life in maybe a negative shape. Ask yourself if this is something that has been experienced by generations in your family tree over and over again. Maybe it's time to break this pattern.

Noticing that there are in fact patterns is the first step. Replacing them with more favourable beliefs and attitudes that you choose consciously now, is the second step of handling this issue. And just like with all the patterns, repetition is what will solidify those new expectations inside of you. While the old thinking might still occasionally manifest as an echo from the past, you will find yourself reacting less and less.

9 · Butterfly
Patience

The notion of metamorphosis of a caterpillar into a butterfly is so familiar to all of us. We may be so focused on that final beautiful, transformed stage, that we often fail to acknowledge the value and importance of seemingly less rewarding, at times unpleasant, or stagnant stages when nothing seems to be happening. As we focus our attention on "nothing is happening" or "I don't like the stage I'm in," all we are doing is slowing the flow of the natural process of transformation. Can you find the beauty and joy in what is here before the colourful wings develop? By constantly chasing the final expression of the butterfly, we are missing the gifts inherent in the current stage of our life, and keeping our focus on what's missing instead of getting the most valuable lessons out of what is already around us. This focus on the missing part can only bring about feelings of dissatisfaction and defeat, and our energy could be best used elsewhere. What's meant for you will not pass you by; you will reach the destination in the most perfect timing. But for now, find ways to appreciate what is.

10 · Zebra
Cycles

The white stripes of the zebra totem are intertwined with the black stripes, teaching us that the dark times help us value and appreciate the happy times. Likewise, the good things in life help remind us that the uncomfortable things won't last forever. Just like the seasons change and the night is replaced by the day, there are cycles in life that keep changing from highs to lows and back to highs again and none of them lasts forever. Take a cue from this impermanent nature and enjoy the good things in your life full heartedly, knowing that they may one day pass. Face the hardships in life with solace and hope, also knowing that they too shall pass.

11 · Kiwi
Nature

The kiwi totem reminds us of the infinite healing and loving power of nature. Taking time to be alone with the trees, walking on the grass barefoot, listening to the song of the river, being lulled by the wind; all of this has a restorative, cleansing power on our well-being. When overwhelmed or stressed, with physical pressure and repetitive thoughts on a loop, turn to a quiet communion with nature to bring back inner balance and clarity. Reconnect with the restorative vibration of your true inner core, unencumbered by the outer distractions. For you too are part of nature.

12 · Brown Bear
Strength

The brown bear totem reminds you of how incredibly strong and powerful you are. You survived your childhood, you survived all the weight of your circumstances, you made it this far. Even though you might wear scars left by your experiences, you ultimately did overcome them and came out stronger and wiser than before. Even if the pressure seems unmanageable right now, know that you have the strength to get up and channel your inner authentic power to help you get through anything. You can do this. But also, just like the bear, at times you might need to hibernate indefinitely, until you gather all the little bits of yourself into the powerful human force that you are.

13 · Hawk
Perspective

The hawk spirit views things from a higher perspective and activates a neutral internal observer. All the obstacles and troubles seem small but also interconnected. All of them when viewed from above seem to lead us to where we are meant to be going. All of the past issues brought us into the now; all of the present and future ones will bring us where we intend to go. Try to view your circumstances from above, from outside the bubble you are in right now. Not ignoring them, not making them out to be unimportant or non-existent, but rather looking from a more detached place and finding internal acceptance toward what is happening. Is it possible that it all brings you to a better place, to a more vivid experience, to a more authentic you? Try to welcome it all from a place of neutrality, allowing space for all the emotions and feelings that arise, and at the same time embracing what is without resistance, and without creating unnecessary density that might pull you down. Embrace a different perspective to change the energy with which you address the situation, which in turn will alter your response to it, and the resonance of your emotional energy.

14 · Raccoon
Resources

Smart and practical raccoon advises you to take account of all your tools and resources, reminding you that you always have everything you need to take the first step towards resolving your issue. Don't look too far into the future, for it might be unattainable or demand unavailable resources and commitment. This might put an undue pressure on you, stopping you from moving forward instead of giving you encouragement and inspiration. Baby steps, making use of everything that's already at your disposal, and steady consistency is what will carry you forward with ease.

15 · Eel
Go with the Flow

The eel totem reminds us to pay attention to how we feel when we decide upon something or choose to act. If you are acting out of fear, then it is best not to proceed, but instead find your inner balance and neutrality. The actions inspired by fear and anxiety are likely to bring more of the same. If the energy of your solutions feels inspiring, uplifting and hopeful, if you heart is in it—that is a green light to go. For every step will feel energetic and will bring you closer to what you want to experience. Go with the flow of the energy, not against it. Don't try to change the circumstance by force, but rather wait for that perfect moment when you feel empowered. The journey would be lighter and your actions much more impactful and rewarding when you consult your internal compass about how you feel. Don't use your energy, effort and action trying to make up for the lack of flow if you are not feeling it. The flow needs to be present first and with it will come an inspired action. You will no longer be fighting with what is but rather being carried towards what's next.

16 · Sheep
Collective Energies

If you picked the card of the sheep spirit animal you might be going through intense emotions, those that you thought were integrated a long time ago. You might be getting frustrated as to why these feelings are reappearing in your life, when often there isn't even an apparent trigger for them to be manifesting right now. You could be consumed by unimaginable sadness hitting you out of nowhere, or very deep-seated sense of despair, grief or anger. The sheep card speaks of collective emotional body, and the possibility that the emotional charge that you are experiencing right now belongs to your lineage, or community as a whole. As we are all one, we all willingly take on this responsibility of clearing emotions and patterns for the collective and a lot of them do not even require our understanding or rational explanation. They just need to be felt and passed through our emotional body unencumbered, without resistance. Knowing that these emotional states will pass as suddenly as they appeared will help you maintain neutrality as you observe them flowing through your body. Breathe deeply through them; they will be gone soon.

17 · Mammoth
Dream Big

Mammoth spirit animal reminds you of how big and important you are, especially in times of feeling small and unworthy. You are a unique expression of light. Even your very existence here is important. Your feelings and needs are important, your well-being and your dreams are important. The world needs and wants you to succeed and experience your dreams. For every goal that you reach makes it closer and easier to achieve for the rest of us, as achieving it becomes our collective inspiration, experience and memory. So, dream big—you deserve to have everything that you wish for, any adventure that you strive for. The universe is always on your side when you allow it to be.

18 · Cat
Your Body

Cat spirit animal reminds you to embrace and embody your physical form, by connecting with internal feelings and sensations inside your body. We so often reside in our heads that we rarely consult the wisdom of our body. Sleep when it asks for sleep, move when it yearns for physical activity, eat when it calls for nourishment. We question everything with our mental body on autopilot, even in matters that do not concern it. There is an intrinsic wisdom in your body. It knows how to do its job and has been carrying you around your world for so many years. It also has a way of helping you notice any internal issues, energies and emotions that have become stuck inside with no way out, those feelings that you dare not feel, those memories that you dare not look at. Listen to your body, explore the sensations, even the uncomfortable ones. For they all carry a message for you; message of inner hurt denied, and inner cries unheard, that desperately want to communicate with you. As you direct your attention towards your inner energy, you will notice that stuck areas inside your body can often manifest as heat, cold, electricity or magnetism. Your conscious attention helps release these trapped energies from your body.

19 · Giraffe
Self-acceptance

Giraffe spirit animal reminds us to embrace everything that makes us different from our surroundings, which makes us stand out in the crowd. It reminds us to bring love to all the unloved parts of ourselves, all those little things that we are so used to hating or denying, all those parts of ourselves that we were told to reject, parts that didn't fit in. Just like little children, these parts are desperately waiting to be loved and accepted, not by just anyone out there, but by you, first and foremost. Every single one of these denied parts carries gifts with them once embraced and accepted unconditionally.

20 · Phoenix
Darkness

Phoenix totem speaks of the dark night of the soul and all the gifts that follow. The night is always darkest just before the dawn, so you might feel you are in the deepest turmoil and there's no light at the end of this tunnel. Then suddenly, everything turns inside out, and you are shown all the lessons and blessings that come after everything that no longer serves gets burned down into ashes, leading you and your life into unimaginable transformation. Trust your internal process of evolution and welcome it without resistance. Look at it as a gift, even for a brief second, and it will be an easier and smoother process to go through.

21 · Wolf
Stories

Wolf spirit animal reminds us to be mindful of where we are spending our energy. Be aware and vigilant of which programs and beliefs you are feeding with your attention and emotions, and which you are starving. When emotions arise, observe them and let them pass through you instead of attaching yourself to the story that brought them about and perpetuating it, anchoring it in your life even more. Whatever situation caused uncomfortable feelings, observe it. Try to figure out the energetic pattern behind it that keeps reappearing in your life, then replace it with a different narrative. Try not to deny those uncomfortable emotions as they come, but rather let go of the story that brought them about. Then, write a different new story to follow, creating a benevolent new pattern to replace the old one. Become the conscious creator of the new chapter of your life.

22 · Crocodile
Release

Crocodile spirit animal deals with the need to retreat to the safety of inner space when overwhelmed with heavy emotions and avoiding tornadoes on the outside. Transmute this powerful energy, allow the emotions to pass safely, dedicating your full attention to your internal state. Don't waste this valuable energy on "fixing" others or circumstances. Their purpose was to bring out the feelings in you, to make you aware of what you've had inside of you for a really long time. Rather than reinforcing the story of what brought about the feelings, focus on feeling them fully, giving your undivided attention and releasing them, with all the lessons and gifts that follow this release. There is an immense value in crying, as it allows the old chemistry to leave your body, creating space for something new.

23 · Armadillo
Boundaries

Armadillo spirit animal card is about staying strong within your power and maintaining healthy boundaries and energetic hygiene.

Keep your awareness on how the outside world is affecting you, how food, drink, music, movies, images, conversation topics and discussions make you feel and protect yourself from whatever doesn't resonate with you. Notice when you are being a people-pleaser for the sake of keeping the peace on the outside but at the cost of your internal well-being and sense of self-worth. Claim your sovereignty and assert your needs and personal space when the situation calls for it.

24 • Oyster
Manifestation

Oyster spirit animal reminds us that all manifestations start on the inside. What you nourish on the inside never fails to manifest on the outside. Anchor the energetic imprint of what you want to achieve by envisioning how it would feel. Use your imagination to bring out the emotional response on the inside, revelling in the positive feelings that accompany the image. However, take care not to attach yourself to these details and not to worry about the how, for the process will reveal itself in time, as well as all the minute details. Attaching yourself to the specific ideas instead of the general feeling, might potentially make you miss the right road or reject the new offering that might be better than you could have ever imagined. Feed this feeling with your imagination, but at the same time try to remain open to the when and the how. The power is in you. Your conscious focus will either lock you in the same old story or release you from the cage of old patterns.

25 · Sloth
Slow Down

Sloth spirit animal serves as a reminder to enjoy the little things in life, slowly and mindfully. We often spend so much time planning for what's next, rushing ahead, that we fail to acknowledge and cherish what is already around us. There's so much beauty and richness in the present moment, in the physical world, in all our senses, in the simple things in life. Don't let all this treasure of the now moment slip away without giving it the attention it deserves, and finding precious joyful moments and positive energy in simple, everyday things. Sloth card inspires slow and thorough enjoyment of things that bring you pleasure. Try to fit into your daily life personal moments of doing something that is not meant to bring you anywhere, just something that you happen to enjoy for the sheer pleasure of it. Keep your inner sloth happy.

26 · Sea Turtle
Ho'oponopono

Sea turtle spirit animal reminds us about the healing beauty of the Ho'oponopono process. Saying internally "I'm sorry, I love you, please forgive me, thank you" to yourself, to others, to the world and circumstances, has the power to change your energy dramatically and can help you "jump timelines" in no time. Gratitude and acceptance dissolve the energy of resistance that keeps you locked in what was. This beautiful ritual can soften any rough edges around the uncomfortable feelings of guilt or regret that are running strong in your life right now.

27 · Seal/Selkie
Longings

Seal shapeshifter, Selkie, speaks of our innermost desires and longings, which we can't help but feel emanating from our soul. You do not need any rational explanation for them. You do not need to provide mental justifications for them, or concern yourself with the ways these desires come about. You know you have them in your heart and they are meant for you. You don't need to explain yourself to anyone, not even to your own mind. Own up to these feelings of longing; they are in you for a reason. Follow your heart no matter how illogical it might seem. You know this inner truth and you don't need any validation to make yourself more certain, for you already feel it.

28 · Mouse-Deer
Self-care

Mouse-Deer card calls for self-love and self-care when it comes to stressful times in your life. Take a break when you need to, even if you have a lot of responsibilities and work. You will be of no use to anyone if you are stressed out and your physical energy is low. You will deal with things better when refreshed and rested. Do not let the stress overpower you; find a little sanctuary in space and time. The world will look after itself while you are providing yourself much needed self-care.

29 · Dove
Forgiveness

The dove card speaks about unconditional love and acceptance. We don't know the full story of others, all the hardships and difficulties that formed their character and influenced their behaviour. We don't know the real deep-seated emotional reasons for their actions and words. Dove totem reminds us to nurture a compassionate part of ourselves that can forgive and accept others, no matter what. Most importantly forgive, accept and love ourselves, despite all the flaws and mistakes that we've made in the past and will make in the future. Love the humanness in you and others.

30 · Fox
Empowerment

The wit and wisdom of the fox archetype calls upon us to find the benefits and advantages in even the most unfavourable circumstances. Can you try to see the good in the perceived bad? Can you accept the possibility of benevolence in whatever hardship you are going through? Contemplating this will inevitably change your attitude from victimhood to empowerment, which in turn will make it much easier to move to a better vibrational place than the one you are currently in.

31 · Snake
Divine Timing

Snake spirit energy speaks of transformation. It comes in its own time and it draws its own specific circumstances. You can't force it to happen, you can't make it come about faster, and you can't slow it down when it does appear. There is a divine timing for everything and pushing against it only causes internal turmoil. Snake reminds us to take everything in our stride with calmness and neutrality, riding the waves of life while holding the knowledge that all occurrences are purposeful. All the players in these events have their purpose too. This card speaks of respecting divine timing and relinquishing control of when something should take place. When things do start to happen, the snake card is a reminder to let go of the old, so that the new can emerge, just like the snake sheds its old skin.

32 · Spider
Patterns

The patterns that we create in our lives by continually feeding them with our emotions and focus, consciously or unconsciously, are "sticky" and cyclical. They tend to come back to us time and time again with new sets of players and circumstances, but causing us to experience the same strong emotions. At times we end up feeling disempowered and trapped by those patterns. As you do your internal work with old emotional charges and release them, you might notice that the old pattern comes back to fill itself up with the old pain, looking for a regular dose of your energy that you are used to giving to it. When you know the work is already done and the old energetic charge is released, it's time to consciously release this pattern and stop reveling in the old addictive painful projections and fears. Take this opportunity to build a new energetic framework by not participating in the old familiar ways. Instead, replace them with the energy of what you are ready to experience instead.

33 · Ugly Duckling
Discernment

If you picked this card then it might be a sign that this is not your time, not your place, or not your team, and it is okay. Don't try to mould what's not yours into your vision just because it remotely resembles what you are striving for. Be discerning. Do not settle for less and forcefully chain yourself to something that doesn't fully resonate just because it seems to be accessible right now. The events, people or experiences you are looking for will come, and they will feel as if they are uniquely tailored to you and would not require any compromising on your behalf.

34 · Polar Bear
Quality

Polar bear card reminds us that sometimes less is more. It encourages us to choose quality over quantity. Take joy in what is already there in your life instead of constantly striving for new experiences and failing to fully immerse yourself in them, while dreaming about the next big thing that will make you happy. At times we use "more" to medicate an internal feeling of anxiety. This feeling just like all the others, needs to be felt, seen and heard. Empty space contains in it more possibilities than the one that's already filled.

35 · Ladybird
Recovery

Ladybird card's intention is to sooth our feelings when it comes to lack, loss, separation, and events that we perceive as negative. Allowing yourself time and space to grieve losses and endings is important. Just like the end of the old chapter is not going to last forever, we are also reminded that something new is being born for us behind the scenes. The events are lining up to match our dreams and to form a new chapter of great adventures. Do not lose hope. Try to see if there is any lesson or value that you can take from the current situation. Perhaps it made you more compassionate or taught you to cherish the good things when you have them. For without the dark it would be hard to define and appreciate what light is.

36 · Dolphin
Friendship

Dolphin spirit animal reminds us of the friendship energy and asks us to look at our life events and people around us with friendly eyes. Sometimes, we are in a place where it's hard to do that, or even impossible. But maybe there is a small part of you that can look at the world with kinder eyes? What if your universe was friendly? While contemplating this thought observe your energy and notice how your inner child becomes more playful and inspired for more fun adventures, as opposed to the feeling of the unmovable forces heavily set against you. Your optimistic gaze towards the world will light up the playful spark and create an opportunity for shared joyful experiences.

37 · Bumblesheep
Wonder

This magical creature wants you to expect the unexpected and to have a little pocket of energy within your field that is ready to receive something extraordinarily magical that defies all explanation yet fits so perfectly and ticks all the boxes! Tune into the energy of this quirky and wondrous feeling to create a little space for your own personal bumblesheep to land at your doorstep.

38 · Reindeer
Worthy

Reindeer totem asks you to notice when and where you see the grass as greener on the other side. It's often so inspiring to observe the highlights of other people's lives and achievements, that we might decide that our way, our life, our craft, our self-expression is not as wonderful and glorious as the results that we see others achieve. Reindeer reminds us that every path is valid, every creation is worthy, and every step of your journey is just as important as those shiny examples that you get inspired by.

39 · Ferret
Royalty

You picked the ferret card because you needed a reminder that you are the royalty of your world. You are the monarch of the place where you live, whether it's a small room or an enormous castle. You are the king of your thoughts and what goes on in your head. You are the queen of your body and what you feel inside of it. You are a little prince of all your inspirations that call you to new experiences. You are a little princess of all the wonderful things that come out of your imagination. Tune into this exalted feeling of self-reverence and notice how the energy of the world around you changes. You are the sovereign of your life.

40 · Comet Moth
Shadow Work

Comet moth speaks of dark shadow feelings and our desire to move away from them and reach for the light. However, sometimes the only sure way out is through the shadows. This card is a reminder of how fleeting these dark feelings can be if we summon the courage to look at them directly. Sometimes, in the midst of very strong emotions we might feel the need to resist them, run away, and avoid the persistent uncomfortable feelings. By not allowing our feelings to just be felt we are actually perpetuating them by attaching stories to them, turning them into enemies and protecting ourselves by all sorts of numbing activities. All these feelings just want to be felt observed and acknowledged. Hold the space for them, allow them to be, and they will share their important messages. Then, they will be out of your system until it's time for them to make an appearance again. None of them lasts forever, even if it feels like that sometimes.

41 · Secretary Bird
Rewrite

Secretary bird totem reminds you to consciously rewrite and edit your personal history. Sometimes, we can get stuck in a certain narrative pattern that leaves us feeling hurt or unhappy. If this story gets too loud, we might start looping and repeating it over and over, while the feelings we experienced in the past remain strong and active in our current vibration. When the realization of this repeated pattern arises, it is time to consciously add a new chapter to the old story. Validating the old history and the feelings is important, and seeing the old pattern from a different lens does not negate the unpleasant parts. We are simply being asked to find a different angle for looking at what happened, adding a little bit to the old history, and ever so slightly changing the pattern that we weave. We can't undo the unpleasant parts, but we can try weaving them into something that will honour the beauty of our personal history.

42 · Hummingbird
Lightness of Being

Hummingbird totem reminds you to take things lightly when events don't go your way, or you don't get something that you've invested a lot of energy into. People don't always reciprocate the care and feelings you shared with them. Yet, no debt ever goes unpaid, no energy is ever wasted. The returns can come to you from different sources and at different times. Letting go of the need for immediate direct payback releases the life energy and gives it wings. The innate knowledge that all good will come back to you in due course will free you from expectations and allow you to enjoy giving, when the time is right for it, rather than doing something with hopes of returns.

About the Artist

Tanya Bond (aka Tatiana Bondareva) is a contemporary artist, teacher and astrologer, who lives and works in the beautiful Irish Midlands. In her portraits Tanya strives to capture genuine emotion and hopes to invite the viewer's imagination into the untold stories of her characters. Her original paintings, prints and colouring books are enjoyed around the world. This is Tanya's second oracle deck, following her self-published Duality Deck.

www.tanyabond.com

https://www.facebook.com/TanyasCharmingCreatures

https://www.instagram.com/tanyabondart/

Notes

For our complete line of tarot decks, books, meditation and yoga cards, oracle sets, and other inspirational products, please visit our website:

www.usgamesinc.com

Follow us on:

U.S. GAMES SYSTEMS, INC.
179 Ludlow Street
Stamford, CT 06902 USA
Phone: 203-353-8400
Order Desk: 800-544-2637
FAX: 203-353-8431